Inhalt English – Sprachkurs

D1723919

1 Arizona | Barbecue

In Arizona treffen sich Freunde zum Grillen. Sie unterhalten sich und warten, bis das Fleisch gar ist.

■ Here are the drinks, guys. Enjoy!

Thank you!

■ Hi, Melissa! Hi, Greg! How are you?

■ Hi, Jimmy! We're fine, how about you?

■ I'm great. This is my girlfriend, Luisa.

Hello! Nice to meet you!

Nice to meet you, too. Where are you from?

■ I'm from Montana.

Oh, Montana is beautiful! I love Montana.

■ Hey, where are Carey and Mike?

Oh, Carey's sick. And Mike's in the office.

■ What a workaholic! So, what would you like to drink?

Um, I'd like an orange juice.

■ And a margarita for me, please.

■ OK.

■ Hey, what's that?

It's salsa. And here are the chips.

■ Oh, wonderful, I love chips and salsa. I'm so hungry! Are you?

Oh, yes! I'm ready to eat!

The steaks and burgers are ready, folks!

---

girlfriend: Freundin
sick: krank
workaholic: Arbeitstier
orange juice: Orangensaft
salsa: würzige Soße aus Tomaten

In dieser spannenden Szene treffen die Familien Clanton und Earp zum letzten Mal aufeinander. **Wyatt Earp**, Sheriff von Silverstone, verteidigt seine Stadt gegen **Ike Clanton** und **Billy the Kid**.

■ Everything in Tombstone is calm and quiet. But on Main Street, there are voices ...

■ Wyatt, where are you? I know you're here!

▨ Who are you? What do you want?

■ You know me. And you know my friends, too.

▨ Oh, he thinks he's clever! What's your name?

■ My name's Ike, Ike Clanton. I come from the town of Silverstone. Does that ring a bell?

▨ Outlaws aren't welcome in our town. And my men and I protect the people of Tombstone. Get the hell out of here!

▨ Hey, why is your arm in your jacket? Watch out! Do you see my gun?

▨ Yeah, I see it. But I tell people only once that they're not welcome here. Are you ready, Doc?

▨ Yeah.

▨ Here's what you want! So, are you satisfied now?

---

calm: ruhig
voice: Stimme
Does that ring a bell?: Erinnert dich das an etwas?
outlaw: Bandit
to watch out: aufpassen
gun: Waffe
satisfied: zufrieden

---

3 Arizona | Sun City

Homer und **Marge** sind von Indianapolis nach Sun City gezogen, um ihr Rentnerdasein in der Wärme zu genießen. Sie haben ein neues Auto, doch Homer trauert dem alten nach. Marge versucht, ihm die Vorteile von Sun City schmackhaft zu machen.

■ Well, Marge, what do you think of our new car?

▨ Oh Homer, come on, these cars aren't that bad. In fact, they're perfect for Sun City. They aren't very expensive, and they have air conditioning, too!

■ Ha ha, very funny! I still miss my Corvette! Now, that was a real driving machine!

▨ Your Corvette is not here. People just don't roar around Sun City in fancy sports cars! We left Indianapolis to relax in the nice, warm weather. Remember? Besides, we're senior citizens now. This car is perfect for our life in Sun City. And at least it's a convertible!

■ You're right, you're right. I just love this car. It's great. It's cheap. And it's safe, too.

▨ Oh, Homer … So, who are the new neighbors?

■ Their names are Betty and Fred. They're from Rhode Island. It's their first year in Arizona.

▨ Really? What do they do here?

■ Well, Betty is a singer in the church choir. I believe her sister's actually the flute player. And Fred likes to garden.

▨ Oh, that's fun! You know, Sun City is a great community. We have a nice house, and the swimming pool is nice, too! And we're together and we're healthy …

■ Yeah, yeah, and I'm a race car driver! Where's the freeway? Ahh … now I know what that sign means!

---

air conditioning: Klimaanlage
to roar around: herumbrausen
senior citizen: Rentner
convertible: Kabriolett
to garden: im Garten arbeiten
healthy: gesund
sign: Schild

Sara und ihr Freund planen eine ausgefallene Geburtstagsfeier für Jerry. Sie reden darüber, wer alles kommen wird. Die Gästeliste ist lang und die Party wird sicherlich ein gelungenes Fest.

■ Hi, Sara. Nice to see you. Can we talk about Jerry's surprise party now?

■ Yes, I have my notes here. This is the information that I have so far. A total of twenty people are on the list. Fifteen are coming to the party. The other five are sad to miss the surprise, but they can't make it.

■ What about Jerry's aunt? The one who's always sick?

■ Aunt Mildred? Oh, she's usually sleepy, not sick.

■ Oh. But you know who I'm talking about, right?

■ Oh yes, I do. But she can't come. She's in Phoenix. Her daughter Kate is coming and bringing a friend. Oh, and Jerry's Aunt Maria won't be there. But her husband is coming.

■ Okay. That's four people. What about Jerry's brother and his sisters?

■ Well, Jerry's brother David is coming. He was very happy to get the invitation. He and his wife are driving from Tucson. And Jerry's sisters are calling tonight to give me an answer.

■ What about –

■ Um … Hold on! I'm making a note about the sisters.

■ Sorry. Who else is joining us?

■ Well, five of Jerry's friends are coming. They're all bringing food.

■ Great! That means less work for us. Uh-oh, I have to go. I have a meeting.

■ Oh, sure. Call me tonight so we can finish planning everything, okay?

---

so far: bisher
invitation: Einladung
Hold on!: Warte mal!
to join sb: jmdm. Gesellschaft leisten

5 New York | Cab drivers

Ein **Taxifahrer** ist neu in New York und möchte von seinem **Kollegen** Wichtiges über die Stadt erfahren. Der nette Kollege erzählt ihm, was er wissen muss, um es in New York zu etwas zu bringen.

■ Hey Buddy, do you have a minute?

▨ Sure. What's up, man?

■ This is my first week in New York and I need some information. Can I ask you some questions?

▨ Go ahead, man.

■ People ask me so many questions and I don't know the answers. But I always try to help. It helps when they think about my tip, you know? So, my question is: What's the highest building in town?

▨ The Empire State Building is the highest building in town. But the highest building in the country is the Sears Tower in Chicago.

■ Oh, yeah, of course. And many tourists also want to know where they can find a nice hotel. Do you know any nice hotels?

▨ Yeah, man. There are a lot of nice hotels in town. Of course, some are nicer than others. But the nicest hotel is called 'Garden of Eden.' I know that because my brother's the owner. It's on 147th Street. Tell your customers to go there.

■ Oh, I understand now. And are there any funny sights in town?

▨ Well, I think the funniest building is the Flatiron Building on Broadway. I don't know any funnier buildings. My father says it's the funniest building in town, too. And he's a tour guide. By the way, he's a good tour guide, maybe even the best! The name of the tour is 'Eddy's tour.'

■ Ah. I understand. Um, here's another question: Can you tell me the shortest way from Manhattan to JFK?

■ Well, there is a short way. But I always take the longest way. Tourists don't know the short way and you can make more money on the long way. Understand?

buddy:	*Kumpel*
What's up?:	*Was gibt's?*
question:	*Frage*
tip:	*Trinkgeld*
building:	*Gebäude*
owner:	*Eigentümer*
sight:	*Sehenswürdigkeit*

6 New York | Chinatown

Mary geht einkaufen, denn sie braucht jede Menge Obst und Gemüse. Bei Dave, dem freundlichen Gemüsehändler, findet sie alles, was sie braucht.

■ Hi.

▨ May I help you?

■ Do you have any parsley?

▨ No, I'm sorry, I don't have any parsley today.

■ Oh. Well, is the garlic fresh?

▨ Of course. All the fruits and vegetables are fresh. The garlic is from New Mexico and it's only $1.25 per pound today.

■ Good. I'll take some then. Could you give me 4 or 5 large bulbs, please?

▨ Sure. Anything else?

■ Um, is that spinach?

▨ Yes.

■ Where does it come from this time of year?

▨ It's from Georgia. Would you like some?

■ Yes, please.

▨ You can go ahead and choose your own. Shall I give you a bag?

■ Yes, please.

▨ Would you hand me the bag, please? I'll just weigh that for you.

■ Here you go. Do you have any sweet apples?

▨ Well, these apples here are sweet.

■ Okay. Would you give me three pounds, please?

▨ Of course.

■ How long do they stay fresh?

▨ In the refrigerator they should stay fresh for a couple of weeks. But don't keep them in a warm place. I can't guarantee they'll stay juicy then. Anything else?

■ No, I think that's it for now.

■ Okay then. That comes to $2.75.
  Out of three ... here's your change.
  Thanks. Have a nice day!

■ Thank you. Bye-bye.

---

parsley: Petersilie
garlic: Knoblauch
vegetable: Gemüse
bulb: Knolle
spinach: Spinat
to choose: auswählen
refrigerator: Kühlschrank
juicy: saftig

In New York sucht eine Touristin aus Idaho das Empire State Building. Ein netter New Yorker erteilt ihr Auskunft und gibt ihr gleich noch ein paar gute Tipps. Und auch sein Hund ist so charmant wie sein Herrchen.

■ Excuse me, can you tell me where the Empire State Building is?

▨ Oh, sure. You're not from here, are you?

■ No, I'm from Idaho. I'm only here for the weekend.

▨ Oh, really? So that's why you're sightseeing in the dark! Let me see your map. Okay. We're here at the corner of Broadway and 47th Street. The Empire State Building is on 5th Avenue and 34th Street. Just walk this way along 47th. After 2 blocks, turn right on 5th Avenue. Walk past the public library until you get to 34th Street. The Empire State Building is on your right. The main entrance is on 5th Avenue.

■ Great. Are there any other places I should see?

▨ Oh, yes. There are lots of interesting places in New York. I think the Guggenheim Museum and the Metropolitan Museum are just as interesting as the Empire State Building. But the most interesting place for me is Ellis Island.

■ Really? How do I get to Ellis Island?

▨ That's easy. Take a cab to Battery Park. The ferry terminal is right at the end of the parking lot. Just buy a ticket to Ellis Island and ask for the schedule.

■ Do you get a good view of the Manhattan skyline from the ferry?

▨ Oh yeah. But you get a better view from the Staten Island Ferry. And the view of Miss Liberty is as good as the view of Manhattan. Of course, it's even more spectacular at sundown.

■ Well, thanks a lot. I really appreciate your help. Oh, is that your dog? He's cute.

▨ Yes. His name is Woodrow.

- Hi, Woodrow, you're such a nice dog. Thanks again.
- You're very welcome.
- Bye-bye.
- Bye now. Enjoy New York!

corner:	*Ecke*
along:	*entlang*
to turn:	*abbiegen*
main entrance:	*Haupteingang*
ferry terminal:	*Fährhafen*
parking lot:	*Parkplatz*
view:	*Aussicht*
to appreciate sth:	*etw. zu schätzen wissen*
cute:	*niedlich*

8 New York | Hot dog stand

Jeden Tag geht Dennis an Dougs Imbiss vorbei und kauft sich einen Hotdog. Dafür hat er nämlich eine große Schwäche. Diesem Hotdog-Abenteuer kann Dennis auch heute nicht widerstehen und unterhält sich ein wenig mit Doug.

■ Hi Doug, how are you today?

■ Hey, Dennis! How are you doing?

■ I'm starving. Can I have a hot dog, please?

■ Sure. Anything else?

■ Well, I'm pretty hungry, and those pretzels there look really good. Maybe I should get something to eat for later? You know, a snack. Yeah! Give me one of those pretzels, too!

■ No problem. I'm afraid the buns are in the oven. Just a minute, okay?

■ Great. Nothing tastes better than a fresh hot dog on a nice hot bun! You know, I think I walk past your stand almost every day.

■ You do, man! You're one of my best customers!

■ Well, I love hot dogs! And when I walk past, I just have to buy one!

■ Ah! I think they're done now. Are you ready for one of the best hot dogs of all time?

■ Am I ever! Hey, where's the ketchup, anyway?

■ It's over there, behind the soda.

■ Great! I love lots of ketchup! And mustard. Ah! There it is, next to the ketchup!

■ Do you want relish on your hot dog too?

■ No, thanks. But I do want something to drink.

■ The soda is right there in front of you. Can I put all of this in a bag for you?

■ Yeah. Oh, and can you put in a napkin and a straw too, please?

■ Of course. How's your wife by the way? Tell her hello from me.

■ Certainly! How much do I owe you?

▓ That'll be four dollars and seventy-five cents, please.

■ Here you go. Thanks. Have a great day, Doug!

▓ Thanks. See you tomorrow, Dennis!

---

pretzel: Brezel
bun: Brötchen
oven: Ofen
to walk past: vorbeilaufen
mustard: Senf
relish: Gewürzsoße
bag: Tüte
napkin: Serviette
straw: Strohhalm
to owe sb sth: jmdm. etw. schulden

---

9 Atlanta | Coca-Cola

Malcolm und Robert sind Fremden-
führer in der Zentrale von Coca-Cola
in Atlanta. Sie erzählen sich Geschich-
ten aus ihrem Arbeitstag und vom
Wochenende. Um sich zu erholen
und fit zu bleiben, verabreden sie sich
zu einer Partie Squash.

■ Hi Malcolm, how was your day?

■ Oh, it was pretty boring. Just a couple of families and a group of 15 school kids. But, you know, those kids were unbelievable! They asked for one cup of soda after the other. Each kid managed to drink more soda than all the other people together.

■ Wow! That's more than I drink in a year! But I sure could use a cup right now!

■ Yeah. Hey, how was your weekend?

■ Oh, it was fun! My wife and I rented an RV and we stayed at the beach for two days. The weather wasn't so good, but we enjoyed the beach just the same. What did you do?

■ We stayed in town. My parents were here from Louisiana. And, believe it or not, my dad wanted to tour Coca-Cola. So, I showed him around on Saturday.

■ Must be nice to work on Saturdays! And, did he like it?

■ Oh, yeah. He loved it. He especially loved the free soda.

■ Of course. Say, do you want to play squash tonight?

■ Yes. Sounds great. I think I'm a little rusty, though. I usually play squash every week but last week I was sick. I haven't played in two weeks.

■ What's a good time for you?

■ Hmm. How about 7:30?

■ Great! Let's meet at the courts.

■ All right. See you then!

■ See you!

---

boring: langweilig
a couple of: ein paar
soda: Limonade
RV (recreational vehicle):
Wohnmobil

0 Atlanta | Farmers Market

Meg und Bill haben einen kleinen Gemüseladen in Atlanta. Leider ist Meg ziemlich ungeschickt und verursacht so manchen Unfall. Das tut ihr dann jedes Mal sehr leid. Gott sei Dank ist Bill sehr gutmütig. Und eigentlich kann sie ja auch gar nichts dafür.

■ Meg, what's the matter with you?

■ Oh, nothing!

■ You know, the last time you said that, you were lying.

■ Well, to be honest, I just tripped.

■ So?

■ Well, I tripped over a crate of tomatoes. Now they're ruined.

■ So what? Is that all?

■ Well, no. This morning, I dragged a sack of potatoes into the store.

■ You dragged a sack of potatoes into the store. And what happened?

■ Well, I didn't tie up the sack and the potatoes all rolled down the street.

■ Ah. Well, that can happen. Or did you want to tell me something else?

■ Umm … I'm really sorry, but I also dropped the crate with the pumpkins this afternoon. They're all crushed.

■ Well, so am I. I assume there are none left to sell? Well, at least we have enough pumpkin purée for a pumpkin pie and smashed tomatoes for soup. We just don't have any potatoes for dinner!

What's the matter?: Was ist los?
to lie: lügen
to trip: stolpern
crate: Kiste
to drag: schleppen
to tie sth up: etw. festbinden
pumpkin: Kürbis
crushed: zerquetscht
smashed: zerschlagen

---

11 Atlanta | In the park

Suzy fährt gern Inlineskates und **Brad** ist ein leidenschaftlicher Skateboarder. Beim Umherfahren lernen sie sich kennen. Und obwohl sie die jeweils andere Sportart zunächst nicht schätzen, entwickelt sich bald eine Freundschaft.

▨ Hey, watch out! Don't crash into me!

■ Why do you think I'm going to crash? You skateboarders are all the same!

▨ Oh yeah? Well, at least I don't need to wear gloves anymore!

■ My mom made me wear these gloves.

▨ Yeah, well my mom told me what to wear this morning too, but I just waited for her to leave and then got dressed.

■ Did she let you try on the clothes before she bought them? Last week my mom came home with these terrible wool pants!

▨ Ha! That's really funny! I bet you looked great! So, what's your name anyway?

■ My name's Suzy. What's yours?

▨ I'm Brad!

■ Are you new here?

▨ Well, not really. My mom just doesn't let me go skateboarding much. She doesn't like the clothes I wear. Most of the time, I have to wear a suit and tie when I go to school.

■ Wow! You have to wear a suit and tie? I bet you look really silly!

▨ Well, what about you? Do you have to wear a skirt and blouse?

■ No, my mom lets me wear whatever I want. Usually I wear jeans and a T-shirt. And she likes to buy clothes on sale. Like I said, last week she brought home some really ugly things!

▨ Ugh! Where does she go shopping, anyway?

■ Well, sometimes we go to nice department stores, but usually we go where clothes are really cheap!

■ I think it's nice to wear fashionable clothes that you like! We always go shopping at the most expensive shops in town!

■ Lucky you. Clothes shopping with my mom means you just take whatever fits.

■ Hey! My mom is going to be really mad if you crash into me and I get a hole in my pants!

■ Man, are you slow. I'm not going to crash into you. You just watch out for yourself, okay? Skateboarders are really all alike!

---

to crash: *zusammenstoßen*
glove: *Handschuh*
pants: *Hose*
clothes: *Kleidung*
suit and tie: *Anzug und Krawatte*
fashionable: *modisch*
hole: *Loch*

Cathy und ihre Eltern besuchen Cyclorama, ein Bürgerkriegsmuseum. Das Museum heißt Cyclorama wegen des großen, runden Gemäldes, das die 'Schlacht von Atlanta' zeigt.

■ Cathy, they call this museum the Cyclorama because of the big round painting we just looked at, 'The Battle of Atlanta.' And they have other civil war objects, too! This map shows the history of the Civil War. It was the largest, most deadly and most expensive war of the 19th century. Did you know that? It also had the first iron warships!

■ Oh.

■ Yes, and the railroad played an important role, too. Look! That train was used during the Civil War! It's called 'Texas' and it's more than 150 years old. Too bad we can't get closer to it. Hey, it's a steam locomotive! Imagine! People actually had to heat the water with coal to make steam. Can you see the smokestack, honey?

■ Uh-huh.

■ After we finish looking at the exhibit, we can go to the gift shop. You can pick out a model train to take home, okay? You'll learn all about this in school, but it's fun and interesting to be able to see it in a museum, isn't it? And here you don't have to listen to a boring teacher talk all day long!

■ Whatever, Dad!

■ You know honey, there's a lot to learn in this museum. Maybe we should take a guided tour.

■ You're right. I'll walk over to the entrance and see when it begins.

■ I already asked about a guided tour at the visitors information, Tom. They told me the next one begins in one hour.

■ Oh. Well, we can look at a couple more exhibits until then. Hey, I wonder what this is?

■ Gee, I don't know either, but it sure looks interesting. What do you think it might be?

▨ Well, it has to have something to do with the train. The sign there says it's also from the 19th century, but it doesn't say what it is.

■ They really should put better signs on the exhibits. Maybe we can ask our tour guide later.

▨ Oh, look over here, Cathy! This is really interesting. These are some of the things people found at the battlefield, and then donated to the museum.

▨ Oh. Well, they sure look old.

▨ You know, after we leave the museum, we can go look at the battlefield too, okay? Somebody told me that if we're lucky, we can still find old bullets from the Civil War. Doesn't that sound like fun?

▨ Oh, great! Let's do that, Dad. Can we go now?

---

painting: Gemälde
map: Karte
warship: Kriegsschiff
railroad: Eisenbahn
steam locomotive: Dampflokomotive
smokestack: Schornstein
guided tour: Führung
exhibit: Ausstellungsstück
battlefield: Schlachtfeld
to donate: spenden
bullet: Kugel

---

13 Florida | Hemingway

, der Besitzer einer Bar in Florida, kommt einem Besucher sehr bekannt vor. In dieser Szene verrät er, warum er diesen Spitznamen hat und wem er ähnlich sieht.

▨ Ernesto, buddy, give me another beer.

■ Sure, man.

▨ Ernesto? I thought your name was Bill.

■ Yeah, it is. But I guess you haven't heard the story yet, huh?

▨ What story?

■ Well, I've been a bartender in this bar for almost 10 years now. I noticed that a lot of people were taking pictures of me.

▨ Yeah? Why? What's the secret?

■ Well, I asked this guy, and it seems I had a famous 'twin brother.' I'm sure you know him.

▨ Oh? Who's that?

■ He's world famous for his books. And he lived in Key West for quite a while …

▨ Oh … now I understand. You mean Ernest Hemingway, right? So, have you read his books?

■ Nah, I don't read much. But I've heard they're okay. I mean, I've come to like him because his looks have brought me some cash.

▨ How's that?

■ I've studied his life a little and learned to make myself look like him, you know? Now I mix the famous Hemingway daiquiri and tell people all about 'my' life. And it works! They like it and they come back. And now they call me Ernesto.

▨ Hmm. Maybe I could use something like that in my business. So, who do I look like, Ernesto?

■ Hmm … Do you really want to know?

---

bartender: Barkeeper
secret: Geheimnis
it seems: es scheint
twin brother: Zwillingsbruder
looks: Aussehen
to look like sb: jmdm. ähnlich sehen

4 Florida | Gatorland

John und Martha besuchen eine Alligatorenfarm in Südflorida. John hat allerdings ein bisschen Angst, aber Martha ist sehr mutig. Hoffentlich halten die Zäune!

■ Um, are you sure you want to go in there?

▨ Of course! Besides, I heard they have a souvenir shop in there. And I've always dreamed of a genuine alligator leather purse.

■ But Martha, you know I'm not particularly fond of reptiles, right?

▨ Oh, don't be such a coward! They're behind fences anyway!

■ Alright. Somebody has to take the pictures ...

▨ Wow! This one looks like it's just swallowed a cow. Have you already taken a picture of him?

■ Uh, yeah. I've never seen one that fat! They've probably just had their lunch, right?

▨ Yeah. But look! This one hasn't!

■ Oh, God. I've never been so glad to be behind a fence in my whole life!

▨ Oh look at that! Have you ever seen so many alligators in one spot? I'm glad I don't have to walk through there. Looks like hell to me!

■ They're so huge. They must be very old. Alligators grow only one inch per year. That means these boys aren't babies anymore! So, are you ready to go to that souvenir shop now?

▨ You know, now that I've seen them, I don't think I want an alligator leather purse anymore.

---

genuine: echt
leather purse: Lederhandtasche
to be fond of sb or sth: jmdn. oder etw. gern mögen
coward: Feigling
fence: Zaun
to swallow sth: etw. herunterschlucken
huge: riesig

Liz und Lucy üben sich im Golfspielen, aber es läuft nicht besonders gut. Zuerst müssen sie den Golfwagen in Bewegung setzen, und auch jeder Schlag auf dem Feld erfordert höchste Konzentration.

- Hey, Lucy, do you know how these cars work? It's not an automatic, it's a standard. I've never driven a standard before.

- Oh dear. No, I don't know how it works. I've never driven one myself! But there are some instructions on the steering wheel, aren't there?

- Oh, yes. Let's see … Turn the ignition key, shift into the lowest gear and go! Hooray! It works!

- Hey! Drive slowly, Liz. I don't want to crash into another car. … Oh! Liz, please stop, the golf clubs are about to fall out.

- Have you stowed them properly? I don't want to lose them. We need all of them to win.

- Well, I don't think that we have a chance anyway. I know it's Ladies' Day, but there are so many young women who play golf so ambitiously these days! And they play several times a week.

- Well, we've played golf for so many years ourselves. We've much more experience. And experience mostly beats age, doesn't it? Don't worry. All right, Lucy, you have to play this one very carefully. We're way behind, and this is our last chance!

- Don't pressure me! I've played brilliantly so far. Now, I have to concentrate on this stroke.

- Come on, you can do it! Oops! Where did the ball go? Certainly not where you intended it to go!

---

automatic (car): Automatikgetriebe
standard (car): Schaltgetriebe
steering wheel: Lenkrad
ignition key: Zündschlüssel
stroke: Schlag

Larry und seine Freunde planen
einen Angelausflug – allerdings ohne
Larrys Freundin Susan.
Doch wie soll Larry ihr dies
beibringen?

Larry, we really have to get started earlier this time. We need to leave the harbor in ten minutes.

Hey, last time, while you were staring so intently at Susan's legs, I was working efficiently.

She has legs? Oh come on man, you have to talk to her. If we're going to catch any fish today, she just can't come.

Alright, I'll talk to her. Susan! You still here? Didn't you want to go swimming?

Nah, I was waiting for you. I thought we were all going fishing together!

Oh … no, we all thought you wanted to go home earlier today. We didn't bring a fishing pole for you.

I'll just use yours then. Look, I've been practicing! You reel in a fish like this, right? Right, Larry?

More slowly, Susan.

Oh, because you don't want the fish to fight, right?

Yeah. Listen, Susan …

And I checked all the fishing equipment too! That way, we can get out on the water sooner.

Thanks, Susan. I wanted to talk to you about something.

Maybe I'll catch a blue marlin! You can take my picture before we throw it back, right?

Throw it back? Um, Susan … the guys wanted me to tell you …

Hey, can you get my sunscreen? And bring me a beer too, will you? Then I'll be ready to go.

Yeah. I'll be right back, Susan … Oh man! The guys are going to kill me.

---

fishing pole: Angelrute
to reel in: einrollen
equipment: Ausrüstung

---

17 Los Angeles | Charlie Chaplin

Auf den Straßen von Los Angeles wird der unwissende Tourist Brian Opfer der 'Versteckten Kamera' von Charlie Chaplin. Denkt Brian wirklich, dass er so schnell ein bekannter Schauspieler wird?

■ Good evening, ladies and gentlemen! And welcome to the Candid Camera show in Los Angeles. Tonight, I'm trying to hire people for a new movie! And – Oh! Here comes a prospective victim now. Excuse me sir, do you have a minute? We're looking for people who would like to take part in a new movie. You look like the perfect candidate. Would you like to become an actor?

▨ What? An actor? You're kidding! Are you sure you're talking to the right person?

■ Oh yes, I'm absolutely sure I'm talking to the right person. You're exactly the right person for the movie.

▨ Um, what's the movie about?

■ Well, it's about a man who is a little naive and doesn't realize that other people are making fun of him all the time.

▨ Who else is acting in this movie?

■ Oh, lots of famous stars. Have you ever heard of Josie Forester and Anthony Husky?

▨ Oh man. I'm going to be so famous! See Jerry? Somebody has finally discovered me!

■ Here's a description of the movie and the address of the studio.

---

to hire sb: jmdn. einstellen
victim: Opfer
to take part: teilnehmen
You're kidding!: Sie machen wohl Witze!
to make fun of sb: sich über jmdn. lustig machen
to discover: entdecken
description: Beschreibung

8 Los Angeles | Walk of Fame

Wie viele junge Frauen in Hollywood will auch Claudia ein Filmstar werden. Eben hatte sie Probeaufnahmen und ihre Freundin Jodie fragt sie, wie es gelaufen ist. Leider war Claudia nicht besonders erfolgreich.

▨ Was your screen test successful?

◼ Well, it was interesting, but I don't know if it was successful.

▨ So what did you have to do?

◼ When I arrived, the secretary was collecting the résumés. The manager was handing out some forms for the actors to fill in. Then, while the other girls were auditioning, I sat in the waiting room and went over my scene again.

▨ Were you nervous?

◼ Was I nervous? I was shaking like a leaf! It was terrible. And when they finally called me in, my feet were numb. It was awful.

▨ How terrible! Did they like your performance?

◼ What performance? When I walked onto the stage, they were still talking about the last girl. They let me wait

for a couple of minutes. And then they told me to dance to the music the pianist was playing. Dance! It had nothing to do with my scene. They just ignored my scene!

▨ Oh! You know, lots of famous stars went through some sort of disappointment at the beginning of their career. Except maybe for this guy here.

◼ Hmm … do you think it would help to put our hands into his prints?

---

screen test: Probeaufnahme
successful: erfolgreich
résumé: Lebenslauf
to audition: vorsprechen
waiting room: Warteraum
to shake like a leaf: zittern wie Espenlaub
performance: Auftritt
disappointment: Enttäuschung

Holly und Kayla joggen in einem Park in Los Angeles. Holly versucht, ein bisschen abzunehmen, aber bisher leider ohne Erfolg. Kayla gibt Holly einige Gesundheitstipps – und hat auch eine Vermutung, warum Holly nicht abnimmt.

- Oh, Kayla, do you have an idea what else I can do to lose weight?

- What's the matter? You're trying to lose weight?

- Yeah. I'm trying. But I haven't been very successful. I've tried everything in the last couple of weeks. But nothing has worked! I just don't lose any weight.

- Hmm. What have you tried so far?

- Well, you know I've been running daily for months now. And I've been going to the health club for two months, without success. And I've been dieting for weeks. It's a pain.

- You haven't had any hunger attacks?

- Only a terrible craving for hot dogs. But I haven't eaten any junk food since that party at Silvia's.

- Have you been drinking enough water and taking the necessary vitamins and minerals?

- Of course! I can't think of anything I haven't done.

- Huh. Maybe you're just not working out hard enough. You know you have to keep your heart rate above 120 for at least 20 minutes in order to burn fat, right?

- Of course I know that. But I have the impression that I've been gaining weight instead of losing it since I've started my wellness program.

- Well, then there's only one other reason I can think of. Are you sure you're not pregnant?

- Kayla?!

---

to lose weight: abnehmen
health club: Fitnessstudio
It's a pain: Es nervt
craving: Heißhunger
to work out: Sport treiben
to gain weight: zunehmen
pregnant: schwanger

Las Vegas ist berühmt für Blitzhochzeiten und Spielkasinos. In dieser rührenden Szene heiratet **Harry** seine **Traumfrau**. Am Ende hat er auch noch eine phantastische Überraschung für sie!

Here comes the bride!

■ Oh, she's so beautiful!

Dear Marianne, dear Harry, we're gathered here to join you two in holy matrimony. And so I ask you, Marianne: Will you take this man to be your wedded husband? Will you love him and honor him?

▨ Harry, I will love you and honor you and be a good wife.

Dear Harry, will you take Marianne to be your lawfully wedded wife? Will you love her and respect her and take care of her in good times as in bad?

■ Marianne, I will love you and respect you and take care of you as long as I live. I will never leave you alone, and I will always buy you what you desire.

▨ Oh, Harry!

▨ I declare you husband and wife. But before you leave, we'll hear your favorite song.

■ I hope you'll enjoy the music.

▨ Oh, Harry, that's so sweet.

Love me tender ... love me true ... Congratulations, Ma'am!

---

bride: Braut
gathered: versammelt
to be joined in holy matrimony: in den heiligen Stand der Ehe treten
husband: Ehemann
to honor: ehren
wife: Ehefrau
to declare a couple husband and wife: jmdn. zu Mann und Frau erklären
tender: zärtlich

Im Spielkasino in Las Vegas hatte Rachel einen sehr erfolgreichen Tag. Sie erzählt Frank, was sie alles mit dem Gewinn vorhat. Frank hat allerdings ganz andere Pläne für sie.

■ Oh, this is fun! Look! I've won again.

▨ Unbelievable! You sure are a lucky one. Say, what are you going to do with all the money you won?

■ Well, first I'm going to buy a new car. And then I'm going to travel to Australia! I've already bought the ticket.

▨ What are you going to do there?

■ I don't know yet. I'll probably go scuba diving or hiking or maybe both.

▨ Sounds like fun. Say, how much longer are you going to be in Las Vegas?

■ Another two days. I'm leaving for Australia on Monday.

▨ Oh. Did you know that they're having a special here tomorrow? They're going to double the money you win. With your luck, that could mean a lot of money for you!

■ Gee, I don't know. I probably won't gamble any more. I don't want to lose all the money again.

▨ Come on! Just a few games. You can't lose all the money in an hour, can you? And, you know, I'd like to see you again before you leave.

■ Well … Okay. I'll see you tomorrow then.

▨ So, is she going to come back again tomorrow?

▨ Yep, I convinced her. I hope we get some of our money back …

---

to travel: reisen
to go scuba diving: tauchen gehen
to go hiking: wandern gehen
to gamble: um Geld spielen
to lose: verlieren
to convince: überzeugen

2 Las Vegas | Truck stop

Truman und Ramona sind Lkw-Fahrer, die sich auf einer Raststätte treffen. Sie erzählen, wohin sie gerade fahren und was sie befördern.

▨ Hi, Truman, good to see you!

■ Sweet Ramona! How are you doing, girl?

▨ Good. Where are you going? On your way to L.A.?

■ No, San Diego. I've got a load of frozen chicken today. Hey, do you have time for a coffee, gal?

▨ No, I'm leaving in a couple of minutes. They're just checking my tires. As soon as they're done I'm out of here. I'm on my way to San Francisco.

■ Are you driving up Route 99?

▨ Nah. I heard there was an accident between Bakersfield and Delano. The police have closed the road in both directions. Which road are you taking?

■ I don't know yet. It depends on the traffic. It's Memorial Day weekend and it seems that the whole world is on the road.

▨ Yeah, I noticed that. But I'm not driving the whole way today. I'm staying in Barstow overnight. My sister lives there and I haven't seen her for 3 years!

■ Well, I have to get my stuff to San Diego today. And I'm picking up another load tomorrow.

▨ Shoot, Truman! You're pretty busy. Well, see you later and good luck for your trip.

---

load: Ladung
frozen: gefroren
gal: Mädel
to check: prüfen
tire: Reifen
on my way: auf dem Weg
accident: Unfall
to depend on sth: von etw. abhängen

23 Chicago | Street musicians

Archie ist Straßenmusikant mit langjähriger Erfahrung. Jetzt stellte sich heraus, dass sein kleiner Sohn verborgene Talente besitzt. Er erzählt seinem Freund Bub, was an diesem Tag passiert ist.

■ Hey, Archie, how's business going out here today?

■ Hey, man, not so bad. I just discovered my son Benny's talent yesterday.

■ What do you mean? His musical talent?

■ Yeah. He's cool, man. Now I have a real partner!

■ How's that? I didn't know your kid had learned to play an instrument!

■ Well, he hasn't. But yesterday, just after I unpacked my instrument, I had to go back to the car. When I came back, I couldn't believe my eyes! Benny was playing and the radio was on. He had taken my saxophone and was pretending to play the music on the radio.

■ So did he make any money?

■ Oh, yeah. People had already left about 30 bucks in his little hat! And there was still a crowd standing around him. So, after I had collected the money, I joined him. After we'd played for about an hour, we had enough money for the whole week.

■ From rags to riches, huh?

■ Hey man, you never know! You never know.

---

to discover: entdecken
to unpack: auspacken
to pretend: so tun, als ob
buck: Dollar
crowd: Menschenmenge
to collect: sammeln
from rags to riches: vom Tellerwäscher zum Millionär

Al Capone, einer der berühmtesten Gangster aller Zeiten, war in Chicago sehr beliebt. Chris wohnt seit langem in Chicago und erzählt seiner Freundin , warum der Gangster trotz seiner Verbrechen so beliebt war.

■ Do you know anything about Al Capone and Prohibition?

■ Well, when you grow up in the Second City, you learn about Al Capone and his gang in school.

■ Really? Tell me more about him.

■ Lots of people say he was the boss in town. He was born in 1899 and died in 1947. He became famous during Prohibition. When the police finally caught him, he had been selling liquor illegally for years.

■ Huh. But I bet he didn't just sell liquor, did he?

■ Nope. His gang had been fighting another gang in town until the Valentine's Day Massacre happened in 1929. They killed many people. Oh, here! This must be the car he had been driving when the police arrested him.

■ So, what was so spectacular about selling liquor?

■ The law didn't allow people to sell or even drink liquor. It was really hard to get any. But there were certain places where you could get some, called 'Speakeasies.' Insiders knew where those places were.

■ Oh. So how long did it take the police to catch him?

■ When the police finally arrested him, he'd been hiding out for years. They caught him red-handed.

■ Wow! People must have hated him!

■ Oh no, most people didn't really hate Scarface. I mean, can you imagine not being able to have a drink or go into a bar on a Saturday night?

Prohibition: Alkoholverbot
Second City: Spitzname Chicagos
to arrest: festnehmen
to catch sb red-handed: jmdn. auf frischer Tat ertappen

Steven und Mark sind beide Architekten und haben große Pläne, wie sie das Stadtbild Chicagos verändern wollen. Leider fällt es ihnen schwer, einen Arbeitsplatz zu finden, an dem sie ihre fortschrittlichen Ideen verwirklichen können.

■ So here's the building I'd been trying to buy for years before they finally told me it was sold to someone else. I had already planned the renovation and reconstruction works in detail. And then they sold it! The architect who's doing the work now isn't even from the Second City.

■ That's not fair. Why didn't they give a young architect a chance? Do you think you can get another building here in the Loop?

■ Well, it's not so easy for a young and unknown architect. Of course, once you've done one building, it isn't a problem anymore. But until then, they distrust you.

■ So, what are you going to do now?

■ Gee, I don't know. There are several other projects I'm interested in.

Once I've finished with the one I'm doing now, I'll send out applications. Hopefully I'll find something although there aren't many jobs available.

■ Yeah. It's not easy.

■ You know, I might just have to create my own job. Say, don't you think that that building over there needs some work?

---

building: *Gebäude*
Loop: *Geschäftsviertel von Chicago*
unknown: *unbekannt*
to distrust: *misstrauen*
application: *Bewerbung*
available: *zur Verfügung stehen*
to create: *schaffen*

Ein sehr schönes, altes viktoriani-
sches Haus steht zum Verkauf.
Leider ist das Haus ziemlich
renovierungsbedürftig. Jetzt wird es
von einem Paar besichtigt. Werden
sie das Haus kaufen und damit eine
Menge Arbeit auf sich nehmen?

This Victorian style house was built in 1875. Many houses like this can be seen all over New Orleans and especially in the Garden District.

Wow. I really like the big windows and that fancy wooden door!

Yes, this house is the oldest in the neighborhood too, and it's one of my favorites. You're really lucky it's for sale! You know, these houses were built to last. They've survived floods, hurricanes …

I can imagine! Why would anyone want to sell such a beautiful old house?

Well, the owner doesn't have any family. The extra rooms are rented out to students now, but she's old and she wants to lead a quiet life. Apparently, the students don't help the landlady at all with the housework. The laundry piles up in the hallway, dishes are left in the sink and the floor is never swept. A complete mess!

Well, I don't mind a little dust, as long as the house is kept in good condition. Does the house have a garage and a basement?

Well, it's hard to see the garage from here, but it's behind the porch, next to the stairs. The basement was converted into another bedroom.

Oh great, so that room could be rented out! Can we take a closer look? Well, this doesn't look good here! What are these holes in the porch? I hope the house isn't being eaten by termites!

No, no, no, there are no termites, but the house does need to be worked on.

Yes, I can see that the house hasn't been worked on for years. It could really use a fresh coat of paint!

- Yeah, the wood here on the porch is in bad shape and the house does need to be painted, but the walls and windows are in good shape, don't you think?

- Oh, yes. And I just love these old crystal windows! You don't see them very often these days.

- They just need to be washed.

- I really like that big balcony, too! Just imagine having a nice Sunday brunch up there.

- Oh, yes, you could spend the whole day up there relaxing and reading a book! And in the winter you could sit by the fireplace. Do you see the chimney up there on the roof? I'm sure it just needs to be swept.

- The rooms get a lot of sun, don't they? I can't imagine that they need to be heated much. Do the rooms upstairs have fireplaces too?

- The master bedroom upstairs has one, but the other rooms don't. So, what do you think? Do you want to make an offer?

- I really like this house a lot, even though it needs to be worked on. I mean, it has such a long history. A real survivor! Yes, I want it. Where there's a will, there's a way!

---

fancy: ausgefallen
to rent: vermieten
landlady: Hausbesitzerin
laundry: Schmutzwäsche
to pile up: anhäufen
hallway: Flur
sink: Spüle
to sweep: kehren
basement: Keller
porch: Veranda
to convert: umbauen
coat of paint: Farbanstrich
fireplace: Kamin
chimney: Schornstein
master bedroom: großes Schlafzimmer
to make an offer: ein Angebot machen

Der Kapitän hat sein Boot überholt und startklar gemacht. Zac erzählt, was er alles gemacht hat und freut sich auf die vielen Touristen, die kommen werden. Ob er auch Japanisch kann?

▨ Hey Zac! The boat sure looks great.

■ Yeah Bob, they did a great job, didn't they? It was painted and repaired last week. The decks were cleaned. They hadn't seen any soap for years! Now the boat's ready for the summer season.

▨ Yeah. She sure is a pleasure to look at now. Hey, did you hear that a new member of the crew was hired yesterday?

■ Really? What's his name? Do I know him?

▨ No, I don't think so. He worked on the Delta Queen before he was hired by the captain. I don't know him myself. His name's Mike.

■ Well, that's good. We definitely need another hand on board. So, is the trip sold out today?

▨ I'm not sure but I think so. Most of the tickets were sold to a group of Japanese.

■ Great. We'll take the scenic route then. That way, they can take lots of pictures. Hey, was the souvenir store stocked up with all those miniature boats?

▨ I'll check. Is there anything else we need for today's trip?

■ Well, do we have a translator on board? The only Japanese words I know are: 'hai, arigato.' That's probably not enough, eh?

---

soap: *Seife*
pleasure: *Vergnügen*
crew: *Besatzung*
to hire: *einstellen*
scenic route: *Panoramaroute*
to stock up: *auffüllen*
translator: *Übersetzer*
probably: *wahrscheinlich*

Preservation Hall ist eines der bekanntesten Jazzlokale der Welt. Zwei Jazzliebhaber freuen sich darauf, dorthin zu gehen und erzählen, warum Preservation Hall so wichtig ist.

■ Do you think we'll get in this time? I'm so tired of standing in line.

▨ I don't know, Lil. But it's a nice evening and I don't mind this.

■ Bill, do you know when Preservation Hall was built?

▨ No, but it's been used for decades. It's become an institution, and is said to be the place with the most traditional jazz music. After it was built, jazz musicians came together here to play. So the more traditional jazz players finally had a place where they could perform. Traditional jazz was not only born in New Orleans, but it has also been preserved here.

■ But Preservation Hall is also used for other things, right? It looks like it's become a tourist attraction to me!

▨ Yeah. You know, I love jazz. It reminds me of the good old days.

Do you remember all the famous songs ...?

■ Oh, yes! What's your favorite?

▨ My favorite has always been 'When the Saints go marching in ....'

■ Oh, when the Saints go marching in!

▨ The most renowned musicians have played it. There are thousands of versions and I love every single one!

■ Oh, it's our turn! Now, if you'd prefer to sing out here, we could earn some money and go out to eat, too!

---

to get in: hineinkommen
to stand in line: anstehen
I don't mind this: Das macht mir nichts aus
to preserve: bewahren
to remind sb of sth: jmdn. an etw. erinnern
renowned: berühmt
It's our turn: Wir sind an der Reihe

29 New Orleans | Pat O'Brian's

Eine Gruppe von Freunden trifft sich bei Pat O'Brian's, einem sehr beliebten Lokal in New Orleans. Die Cocktails des Hauses sind allerdings mit Vorsicht zu genießen!

■ Pat O'Brian's is a local hot spot, do you like it?

▨ Oh, yes. So what are you having tonight?

■ My favorite! I've already ordered.

Here's your order sir. Let me know if you need anything else.

■ Thanks.

▨ So that's your favorite drink? What's it called?

■ The O'Brian's Breezy Breeze. Soon to be the most popular drink in town. I can see it now ... great distances will be traveled by people who want to try it.

▨ Oh, really?

■ Yeah. The Breezy Breeze will be made famous in no time flat. This small, local bar will be transformed into a popular tourist attraction!

▨ Huh. Before you know it, O'Brian's will be overrun by tourists who read about it in their guide books. Sounds great. I don't know, Seth ...

■ Well, why not? The Breezy Breeze will be known everywhere!

▨ Yeah, but then we'll never be able to get a table when we want one! And the prices will be pushed higher than ever before. You want that?

■ Not really. But look on the positive side. Amazing drinks will be created and made available for your nightly enjoyment! Sweet or sour, garnished with pineapple or cherries. Those drinks will keep customers coming back again and again!

---

hot spot: angesagter Treffpunkt
in no time flat: im Handumdrehen
overrun: überlaufen

30 San Francisco | Cable Car

Ken und Patty haben es nach langem Warten endlich geschafft, einen Platz in einem 'Cable Car' zu ergattern. Während der Fahrt überlegen sie, was sie für die Wanderung am Wochenende brauchen. Wird Ken trotz der Stechmücken mitgehen?

- Oh no, there's a long line! Do you think we'll get a seat?

- Well, if we don't, we'll just have to walk.

- Boy, am I glad we made it. It feels so good to sit, doesn't it?

- Yeah. So, what else do we need for our hike on the weekend?

- Let's see. We'll need a cap and rain gear if it rains. If the sun's out, we'll probably need insect repellent.

- Insect repellent? Patty, are you saying that there are going to be mosquitoes? I don't want to go if there's one single mosquito!

- Oh, Ken, come on, that's ridiculous! You want to stay at home just because of one or two bug bites?

- Yep. How can I enjoy the hike if I have to defend myself against mosquitoes all the time?

- You know what? I've hiked at the El Capitan every year for the last 5 years. And I'm still alive. The mosquitoes are not going to eat you. Are you sure you don't want to go?

- Well, the last time you said there weren't any mosquitoes, I was covered with bites when we got home. And you always have a different excuse. So what's your excuse this time?

- No more excuses. But I'll buy you a beer if you come home with more than five bites, okay? Besides, if you wear those new sunglasses, the mosquitoes won't see you anyway!

- You mean like this? Cool, huh?

---

hike: Wanderung
rain gear: Regenkleidung
insect repellent:
Insektenschutzmittel
mosquito: Stechmücke
bite: Stich

Dave und Kim lieben San Francisco, doch Dave hat ein Jobangebot bekommen, das er nicht ausschlagen kann. Und der neue Job ist in Boston. Kim ist gar nicht glücklich darüber. Was machen sie jetzt?

■ You know, if we stayed in San Francisco, I'd be so much happier. I love it here.

■ I do too, Kim. And I could imagine staying here forever, if my job were more interesting! But if I took the job in Boston, I'd earn twice as much as I do now.

■ I know, I know. And the cost of living is lower there, too.

■ Well, do you think you could you be happy in a new city without a job?

■ No, I don't.

■ But if you got a job in Boston, would you consider moving? I mean, would you at least think about it?

■ Dave, I've worked hard at my company. I don't see it as a job. It's my profession, and you know I take it seriously.

■ I know. So you wouldn't leave even if you had a job in Boston?

■ Oh Dave … Why do we have to move across the country? Can't you find a new job here? If you found a better job here, we wouldn't have to move!

■ That's true. If I had a better job, I'd also be a lot happier! But I need to change jobs now. I can't stay where I am any longer. So, should I take the job in Boston, but keep looking for another position here?

■ No. It'll be easier to find a new job in San Francisco if you stay here. How about something in middle management? That way, we can both stay in the city we love, right?

---

to earn: verdienen
cost of living: Lebenshaltungskosten
to consider: in Betracht ziehen
to move: umziehen
position: Stelle

John besitzt einen Weinberg im Napa Valley und weiß genau, wie man die Weinstöcke pflegen muss, um guten Wein zu erzeugen. Und wie bekommt man nun einen Spitzenwein?

■ All right guys, this is what you have to do. You have to make sure the grapevines are cut the right way.

■ Um, why do the plants have to be pruned so carefully?

■ Well, if they're pruned properly, the limited number of grapes get more water and more nourishment. If the grapevines aren't pruned, you get more grapes, but the quality is not as good.

■ So the quality of the grapes is crucial?

■ Oh yes, and we'll have a good yield this year … unless it rains too much. Of course, if it rains much more, the soil will be saturated and the grapes will start to rot.

■ Oh … So that means that they need an exact amount of water: not too much and not too little?

■ Exactly. Last year, we would've lost all the grapes if the rain hadn't stopped in time. It was close!

■ Huh. So provided that there's enough but not too much rain, the wine will automatically be good, right?

■ Oh, no. It takes much more than that to make a good wine! Actually, the vinification is the most important part of wine making. But the time of the harvest and the storage of the wine are important, too, as well as the use of pesticides.

■ So that's what's in the tank!

■ Yeah. What did you think? We don't run around and catch the bugs with our hands! I think you'll find it's hard enough to apply this stuff to the grapevines. So, let's go boys! This looks like a good wine year for California!

grapevine: Weinstock
to prune: (Pflanzen) stutzen
nourishment: Nährstoffe
crucial: entscheidend
yield: Ernte
saturated: durchnässt
to rot: verfaulen
provided that: vorausgesetzt
vinification: Weinerzeugung
tank: Becken
bug: Ungeziefer

33 Hawaii | Hula show

Touristen sehen sich gern eine 'Hula Show' auf Hawaii an. Aber was ist eine 'Hula Show'? Am besten macht man gleich mit!

■ My guide book gave us great directions! We're right on time.

▦ It's good you brought that book along. It's been a big help. So, what does the guide book say about the actual show?

■ Let's see … The book says that this is one of the most popular hula shows in all of Hawaii. That sounds good, doesn't it? Let's go find our seats, shall we? I want to be able to see what's going on.

▦ Oh, you go ahead. I want to look at some of those stands over there. I need a souvenir for Amy. Do you think Amy will like this necklace?

▦ You know, Mary told me that coral jewelry can be found all over Hawaii. Okay, I'm done. Now we can look for our seats. That sign says we need to go in this direction.

▦ And look, the ladies are just ahead of us looking for the right row now!

■ Wow! It sure feels good to sit down after such a long day, doesn't it?

▦ Oh! It's starting! What does the word 'Hawaii' mean, anyway?

■ Well, my book says that 'Hawaii' is a Polynesian word meaning 'homeland.' And those beautiful, colorful dresses are called 'holokus'. Aren't they pretty?

▦ Sssssshhhhh!

■ Well, you did ask. Oh, my book says that they were first used on the islands in the 1800s. The dresses were introduced by missionaries from New England. The book also notes that hula was originally a religious dance form. How interesting! Hand motions are used in contemporary hula to tell stories about the islands. Did you know that? And those are traditional skirts according to the book, because they're shorter and made of grass.

- Excuse me Mary, but would you please quit talking!

- Come on, Mary! Before you get us in trouble, let's go dance.

- Oh, this is fun! So how do I look?

- Just great, honey.

---

guide book: Reiseführer
necklace: Halskette
dress: Kleid
to introduce: einführen
hand motion: Handbewegung
according to: zufolge
to quit sth: mit etw. aufhören
trouble: Ärger

Am Strand tummeln sich Windsurfer. Einer von ihnen ist ein richtiger Angeber. Schon bald stellt sich aber heraus, dass er doch nicht so gut ist, wie er behauptet.

■ Hi. Nice board. Are you going out?

▨ Yep. I'm going to show my friends how to windsurf.

■ Um, the wind is pretty nasty. Do you think you'll manage?

▨ Oh, I don't mind strong winds. I'm an experienced windsurfer, man. I actually love nasty winds. I've been to places where the wind and the waves were a lot nastier than here!

■ I see. Well, have fun then!

▨ Thanks. See you later, dude.

▨ So, who's that guy in the black suit? He doesn't seem to know what he's doing. It's taken him ten minutes to get on his board and pull the sail out of the water!

■ Yeah, I know. I think he's having problems with the wind. I told him that the wind was pretty nasty. But he said he was an experienced windsurfer.

▨ Really? Oh no! He almost crashed into that other guy! He certainly doesn't look like an experienced windsurfer to me!

■ No, he doesn't. He also said that he'd been to places where the winds and the waves were a lot nastier than here.

▨ Oops! That wave just blew him off the board again! Man! I can't believe it! The wind is perfect and the waves are great today.

■ Yeah. You know what? He said he actually loved strong wind, but he can hardly stay on the board.

▨ Well, maybe he learned windsurfing in a swimming pool.

■ Yeah. In any case, he sure seems to be a Mr. Bigmouth.

■ That's for sure. Oh, hey. I just talked to the lifeguard. He's expecting a storm within the next hour. We better put our equipment in the car.

■ Okay, but let's hurry! I want to see how Mr. Bigmouth manages the storm!

board:	*Brett*
nasty:	*grässlich*
experienced:	*erfahren*
wave:	*Welle*
to crash into sth:	*mit jmdm. zusammenstoßen*
bigmouth:	*Angeber*
lifeguard:	*Rettungsschwimmer*

English – Sprachkurs 1

35 Hawaii | Boogie boarders

Ein paar Freunde liegen am Strand und sehen den Surfern zu. Einer erzählt von seiner Verabredung vom Vorabend, die nicht ganz nach Plan verlaufen ist.

■ Dude, how was your date last night? How'd it go?

▨ Well, Meg had said that she might not be able to come to the beach club. But eventually, she did.

■ Cool. Wow, that's a big wave! And Sean missed it! So, what happened after Meg showed up?

▨ I asked her if she wanted to dance, but she said she couldn't cos she'd hurt her foot on the boogie board that morning. So we just hung out and talked.

■ Hey, look, Sean's giving it another shot. Awesome! So, did you ...?

▨ Uh, no. I put away one drink after the other cos she didn't want to dance. And when I asked her if she wanted to go somewhere else, she said she didn't. So I just kept drinking. I guess you know what happened. I was pretty smashed after a couple of hours.

▨ Hey, Chuckie and Mike. Hey Chuckie, you look wiped, man.

■ Yeah! Dude, I'm starving. Can we go and get something to eat?

▨ Good idea.

▨ So, Chuckie, it was a no show last night, was it?

▨ No man, she was there, but then she got fed up with me, called me a jerk and told me to get lost. No big loss. I had a great time anyway. There was this other girl, Amy ...

▨ Oh! There's a big one! But what's Sean doing? That jerk lost his boogie board! I told him to hold on tight! Aw, let's go eat!

■ Yeah, I'm starving. Let's go.

date: Verabredung
beach: Strand
to hurt: verletzen
to give it another shot: es noch
einmal versuchen
Awesome!: Wahnsinn!
to put away one drink after another:
ein Getränk nach dem anderen
hinunterkippen
smashed: besoffen
to look wiped: fertig aussehen
starving: vor Hunger sterben
to be fed up with sb: die Nase von
jmdm. voll haben
jerk: Blödmann

Notizen